Stacy A. Hagen

Intensive ESL Program
Edmonds Community College

AtEase

A Fluency Builder

Prentice Hall Regents
Englewood Cliffs, N.J. 07632

To Nancy Kennedy
For her priceless gifts of friendship, authenticity, and love.

Library of Congress Cataloging-in-Publication Data

Hagen, Stacy A., 1956–
   At ease: a fluency builder / Stacy A. Hagen.
      p.   cm.
   ISBN 0-13-293077-3
   1. English language—Textbooks for foreign speakers.   I. Title.
PE1128.H224   1995
428.3´4—dc20   94-9559
                                           CIP

Acquisitions Editor: Nancy Baxer
Director of Production and Manufacturing: David Riccardi
Editorial Design/Production Manager: Dominick Mosco
Project Management: J. Carey Publishing Service
Interior Design: J. Carey Publishing Service
Illustrator: Mary Dersch
Cover Design Coordinator: Merle Krumper
Cover Designer: Rosemarie Paccione
Production Coordinator: Raymond Keating

Copyright © 1995 by Prentice Hall Regents
Prentice-Hall, Inc.
A Simon & Schuster Company
Englewood Cliffs, New Jersey 07632

Printed in the United States of America

10 9 8 7 6 5 4 3 2 1

ISBN 0-13-293077-3

Printed on Recycled Paper

Prentice-Hall International (UK) Limited, *London*
Prentice-Hall of Australia Pty. Limited, *Sydney*
Prentice-Hall Canada Inc., *Toronto*
Prentice-Hall Hispanoamericana, S.A., *Mexico*
Prentice-Hall of India Private Limited, *New Delhi*
Prentice-Hall of Japan, Inc., *Tokyo*
Prentice-Hall of Southeast Asia Pte. Ltd., *Singapore*
Editora Prentice-Hall do Brasil, Ltda., *Rio de Janeiro*

Contents

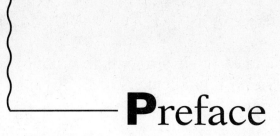

Preface

At Ease: A Fluency Builder provides low to intermediate level students with a variety of activities for extended, yet structured, speaking and discussion. As students work their way toward fluency, they need multiple opportunities for using English. This text provides a variety of high-interest topics that encourage students to take part in discussions, present short talks, solve problems, and interact with each other and English speakers. A highlight of this text is that the topics are based on personal experience rather than global knowledge (nuclear war, poverty, homelessness) so students with a more limited vocabulary can participate in these activities.

The text is divided into four sections:

- Discussions

Students are asked to draw upon their own experiences by exploring such topics as body language, customs, culture shock, and stereotypes about countries.

- Individual Speaking Activities

Preliminary questions guide students toward the creation of their own short talks. By the time they have answered and discussed these questions, they have in effect put together their talk in an encouraging, friendly fashion.

- Interviews

These tasks allow students to practice with each other, interview other speakers of English, and create their own interviews.

- Problem Solving

Students get to solve a mystery, work out a logic puzzle, try several brain teasers, and complete pairwork activities.

A Teacher's Manual has been included in the back of the text with notes for each activity, and answer keys where applicable. I welcome your feedback.

Stacy A. Hagen
Intensive ESL Program
Edmonds Community College
20000 68th Ave. W.
Lynnwood, WA 98036

Acknowledgments

This was a fun book to write, in part because of the creativity and energy of several people who were so generous with their help. My thanks to the following:

Bill Hashbarger of the University of Washington Intensive English Program for the ideas found in the Introductory Activity.

Naser Al-Mehairbi, my lively S/L 4 student, for his help with the brain-teaser activity.

Several of my Speaking/Listening classes at Edmonds Community College for their willingness to try these activities and enthusiasm for them.

Jennifer Carey, Project Manager, for her careful design of the book and friendliness at all stages of production.

Nancy Baxer of Prentice Hall, whose excitement and attention to detail guided this project from start to finish. Her remarkable concern for ESL students and what they enjoy is evident throughout this text.

Introductory
Activity

Getting to Know You

In this activity, you will learn the names of all the students in your class.

1. Sit in a circle.

2. The first person says his/her first name and one reason s/he is studying English. *But the reason cannot be true.*

For example:

I am in this class because I am a movie star.
I want to improve my English for my next movie.

You can say anything you want, but it must be *false*.

3. The second person must repeat the first person's name (not the reason) and then say his/her own name and why s/he is in the class.

4. The third person repeats the names of persons 1 and 2 and then gives his/her name and a reason s/he is in the class.

5. Continue all the way around the circle, each person repeating all the names before and then saying his/her name and a reason. Your teacher will be the last person to speak and say everyone's name.

   Note: If the class has a lot of students, you might want to do ten to fifteen names and then begin again with another group of ten to fifteen.

Variations:

a. Say what kind of car you would like to be and why.

b. Say what animal you would like to be and why.

Unit 1

Discussions

Activity 1

Ideas About a Country

Many people have ideas about a country before they visit. Some are true and some are not. Here are ideas some people have about the United States. Did you hear these before? If you have visited the United States or are in the United States now, do you think they are true (do you agree)?

Part I

Read the list. Check the statements you have heard
before. Check the ones you can agree with.

	heard before	*agree*
1. You need a car.	____	____
2. Most parents are divorced.	____	____
3. Don't wear jewelry. Someone will steal it.	____	____
4. People are superficial (friendly on the outside but not inside).	____	____
5. It's a big country.	____	____
6. There is a lot of freedom.	____	____
7. Teenagers don't respect their parents.	____	____
8. People smile too much.	____	____
9. Taxes are high.	____	____
10. It's a violent country.	____	____
11. Everyone owns a gun.	____	____
12. People are very friendly.	____	____
13. School is very easy.	____	____
14. Food doesn't have flavor (taste).	____	____
15. People eat too much.	____	____

heard
before   *agree*

16. Most teenagers use drugs. ____ ____

17. When kids turn eighteen, parents say "good-bye" and make them leave their house. ____ ____

18. It's an expensive country. ____ ____

19. Women are too strong. The men are weak. ____ ____

20. People say exactly what they think. ____ ____

After you have chosen your answers, discuss them in your small group. Share your answers with the whole class.

Part II

Ideas about _____
(name of a place)

In small groups (people from the same countries together, if possible) make a list of ideas people have about your country or the area where you live. Make copies of the list for your classmates, or write it on the board. See if your classmates have heard the same ideas and if they agree.

heard
before   *agree*

1. _____ ____ ____

2. _____ ____ ____

3. _____ ____ ____

4. _____ ____ ____

*heard
before* *agree*

5. _____ ____ ____

6. _____ ____ ____

7. _____ ____ ____

8. _____ ____ ____

Write any new vocabulary or phrases that you learned in this discussion in the space below.

_____   _____

_____   _____

_____   _____

_____   _____

_____   _____

Activity 2

Body Language

Part I

What body language do you use to show the following in your country? How are these the same or different in an English-speaking country (for example, United States, United Kingdom, Canada, Australia)?

• How do you ask someone to "come here"?
• How do you count to ten in your country?
• How do you show you are confused?
• How do you show you feel good or happy?

- How do you show you understand?
- How do you show you feel angry?
- How do you show you think something is stupid?
- How do you show you are interested in a class?

Part II

In small groups, write a few *ideas* (not complete sentences) for each of the following questions and discuss them.

1. In some cultures it is impolite to look directly at someone. Is this true for your culture? If so, in what situations?

   _____

   _____

   _____

2. How close do people in your country stand to one another? Show the other students. If you are living in another country, how close do you stand to people in that country? If this is different, how does it feel?

   _____

   _____

   _____

3. If a person crosses his/her arms when s/he is talking, does this mean anything? What about if a person takes or touches your arm?

_____

_____

_____

_____

4. Do people in your country think it is good or bad to show emotions (feelings)? Explain your answer with examples.

_____

_____

_____

_____

5. In many cultures, long silences are positive (good). In others, they are negative (not good). What about your country? How do people in your country feel about long silences? If you are living in another country, how do you think people feel about silence? How about in the classroom?

_____

_____

_____

_____

_____

6. If you are living in another country, compare your country with the host country. In which one do people use more gestures (body language)? Explain. Are there any gestures that you think are strange?

_____

_____

_____

_____

Part III

Share your answers with the whole class.

Write any new vocabulary or phrases that you learned in this discussion in the space below.

_____   _____

_____   _____

_____   _____

_____   _____

_____   _____

Activity 3

Dating, Marriage, and Divorce

Part I

In small groups, write a few *ideas* (not complete sentences) for each of the following questions and discuss them.

1. At what age do people in your country begin dating?

   _____

   _____

   _____

2. How do people in your country usually meet each other (through the family, school, friends, blind dates, etc.)?

   _____

   _____

   _____

   _____

3. Where do people usually go on dates? What is an example of a "fun" date? Can the couple go alone, or do they have a chaperone?

_____

_____

_____

_____

4. Tell about marriage in your country. Who makes the decision about marriage? What kind of ceremony or wedding does the couple have? What do people wear? Who pays? How many hours/days is the wedding? Is there a honeymoon? If yes, where do people like to go?

_____

_____

_____

_____

5. Is there a lot of divorce in your country? If yes, what do you think are the reasons? How do you feel about divorce? In some countries, a husband can have more than one wife. Is this true for your country? What do you think about that?

_____

_____

_____

_____

6. If you are living in another country now, what are some ways a person can meet people of the opposite sex? Do you know any useful English phrases for meeting people?

_____

_____

_____

_____

7. Do you think you could marry someone from another culture? Why or why not?

_____

_____

_____

_____

Part II

Share your answers with the whole class.

Write any new vocabulary or phrases that you learned in this discussion in the space below.

_____   _____

_____   _____

_____   _____

_____   _____

_____   _____

Activity 4

Customs

Every country has special customs.

- In Asia, people take off their shoes when they enter a house.
- In some cultures, people eat rice from their hands.
- In the United States, people say "thank you" when they pay a bill.

Part I

In small groups, write a few *ideas* (not complete sentences) for each of the following and discuss them.

1. Think of three customs in your host country that seem strange or different to you. Write them below. (If you are not living in a foreign country, try to think of customs in other countries that you have heard about.)

   a. _____

   b. _____

   c. _____

2. Are there any customs in the host country or another country that you like or would like to have in your country? If so, write them below.

   a. _____

   b. _____

   c. _____

3. Now think of three customs a visitor to your country would find strange or different. Write them below.

a. _____

b. _____

c. _____

Part II

Share your answers with the whole class.

Write any new vocabulary or phrases that you learned in this discussion in the space below.

_____   _____

_____   _____

_____   _____

_____   _____

_____   _____

Activity 5

After Death

Part I

In small groups, write a few *ideas* (not complete sentences) for each of the following and discuss them.

1. In some cultures, people believe that after you die, you are born again as an animal or another person. Other people believe in Heaven and Hell. Some believe you become a spirit or energy. Others believe there is nothing after death.

   Write a few ideas about what you think happens to you after you die.

   _____

   _____

   _____

   _____

   _____

2. Do your actions or behavior in life affect (change) what happens to you after you die? If yes, give examples.

_____

_____

_____

_____

3. What do you do in your country (or in your religion) when someone dies?

_____

_____

_____

4. Is there a special day of the year when you honor (respect) the dead or when the dead return? What do people do?

_____

_____

_____

_____

5. Some people believe in fate. (This means that everything about your life is decided before you are born.) Do you believe in fate? Why or why not?

_____

_____

_____

_____

Part II

Share your answers with the whole class.

Write any new vocabulary or phrases that you learned in this discussion in the space below.

_____   _____

_____   _____

_____   _____

_____   _____

_____   _____

Activity 6

Advantages/ Disadvantages

Learning another language and living in another country can have many advantages (good things). But it can also be difficult and have disadvantages (bad things).

Part I

In small groups, write five advantages (good things) of learning English and/or living in another country. (Students in the same group should agree on the answers.)

a. _____

b. _____

c. _____

d. _____

e. _____

Now write five disadvantages (bad things) about learning English and/or living in another country. (Students in a group should agree on the answers.)

a. _____

b. _____

c. _____

d. _____

e. _____

Part II

Write a few *ideas* (not complete sentences) for each of the following questions and discuss them in your small groups.

1. What do you like best about speaking/learning English?

   _____

   _____

   _____

   _____

   _____

2. What do you like least (opposite of best) about speaking/
   learning English?

   _____

   _____

   _____

   _____

   _____

3. If you are living in another country, what are the best and
   worst things about living there for you?

   _____

   _____

   _____

   _____

4. What are some ways to make friends with native speakers of English? How do visitors to *your country* make friends with native speakers of your language?

_____

_____

_____

_____

5. If a person feels homesick, what are some things s/he can do to feel better? Have you ever felt homesick? Were there things that helped you feel better?

_____

_____

_____

_____

6. If you are in another country, do you feel the same now as when you first came to the host country? How have your feelings changed? How are they the same?

_____

_____

_____

7. Would you recommend that a friend from your country go to another country and learn English? Why or why not?

_____

_____

_____

Part III

Share your answers with the whole class.

Write any new vocabulary or phrases that you learned in this discussion in the space below.

_____   _____

_____   _____

_____   _____

_____   _____

_____   _____

Activity 7

What Makes a Good Partner?

Part I

Form groups of three to five students of the same sex. The women will list five qualities they think would make a man a good partner. The men will also write five qualities that would make a woman a good partner. (Students in a group should agree on the answers.)

a. _____

b. _____

c. _____

d. _____

e. _____

Write your list on the board. Compare and discuss your list with the lists from the other groups.

Part II

Get into small groups (men and women mixed). Write a few *ideas* (not complete sentences) for each of the following questions and discuss them.

1. Who should control the money? Why?

   _____

   _____

   _____

2. Who should do the housework and cooking? Should the couple share these chores? Why or why not?

_____

_____

_____

_____

3. How much freedom should each partner have?

_____

_____

_____

_____

4. Can the woman be smarter than the man or the man smarter than the woman? Explain your answer.

_____

_____

_____

_____

5. In a marriage, can a woman be a good wife and not want to be a mother? Can a man be a good husband and not want to be a father? Explain your answer.

_____

_____

_____

_____

Part III

Share your answers with the whole class.

Write any new vocabulary or phrases that you learned in this discussion in the space below.

_____ _____

_____ _____

_____ _____

_____ _____

_____ _____

Activity 8

The Perfect Job

Part I

In small groups, write a few ideas (not complete sentences) for each of the following questions and discuss them.

1. Here are some jobs:

travel agent	school custodian
architect	accountant
lawyer	secretary
athlete	repair person
singer or rock star	real estate salesperson
actor	nurse
garbage collector	engineer
author	flight attendant
firefighter	police officer
farmer	doctor
teacher	business person
computer engineer	psychologist

What do you think is the best job on the list? Why?

_____

_____

_____

_____

What do you think is the worst job on the list? Why?

_____

_____

_____

_____

2. Is there a job on the list that would be the perfect job for you? If not, what would be the perfect job for you? Why?

_____

_____

_____

_____

3. Are there any jobs on the list that are not good for women or that women are better at? Are there any jobs that are not good for men?

_____

_____

_____

_____

4. What do you think is important for a good job? Money? High status (high place in society)? Happiness? Why?

_____

_____

_____

_____

5. Which is better: a low-paying job and happiness, or a high-paying job you don't like? Why?

_____

_____

_____

_____

6. In your country, if you choose a job (for your career) and you don't like it, what can you do?

_____

_____

_____

_____

Part II

Share your answers with the whole class.

Write any new vocabulary or phrases that you learned in this discussion in the space below.

_____   _____

_____   _____

_____   _____

_____   _____

Activity 9

Culture Shock

When you go to another country, or even a place different from where you live, it can be a big shock to you and to your body. Many things are new and different. You feel a big shock because you are in a new culture and trying to speak a new language. This is called **culture shock**. Culture shock can happen at the beginning, in the middle, or at the end of your stay. Here are some symptoms (signs) of culture shock:

- Eating too much
- Not eating much

- Sleeping a lot
- Not sleeping
- Complaining (I don't like this; I don't like that.)
- Getting angry easily
- Crying more than usual
- Feeling depressed (very, very sad)
- Feeling frustrated (nothing is working for you—you try but can't succeed)
- Thinking "I am a bad person," or "I am a stupid person."
- Feeling homesick
- Thinking everything is wonderful

Part I

In small groups, write a few ideas (not complete sentences) for each of the following questions and discuss them.

1. Have you had culture shock before? Which symptoms did you have? Give examples. If you have not had culture shock, do you know someone who did? What happened to him/her?

   _____

   _____

   _____

2. If you have had culture shock, when did you begin to feel these symptoms (when you first arrived, later in your stay)? How long did they last (continue)? What did you do to change them or feel better?

   _____

   _____

   _____

3. If you had culture shock and complained about the host country, what kinds of things did you complain about?

   _____

   _____

   _____

4. If someone has culture shock, what advice or suggestions could you give them?

_____

_____

_____

5. When someone is living in another country, what are some ways to stay in touch with (not forget) the first language and culture?

_____

_____

_____

Part II

Share your answers with the whole class.

Write any new vocabulary or phrases that you learned in this discussion in the space below.

_____   _____

_____   _____

_____   _____

_____   _____

_____   _____

Activity 10

Crime and Punishment

Part I

Here are a few ideas some people might consider crimes.

- having a gun in your house
- driving a car while drunk
- cheating in business (not being honest)
- spying (getting information about another government; for example, C.I.A. or James Bond)
- robbing a drugstore because you need medicine for your child

- terrorism
- having a boyfriend/girlfriend in addition to your husband/wife
- violence in the family; for example, hitting someone such as your wife or a child
- mercy killing (helping a sick person die)

Are all of these crimes? Check the ones you do not think are crimes. In small groups, discuss why you don't believe they are crimes.

Part II

Write a few *ideas* (not complete sentences) for each of the following questions and discuss them.

1. Choose two or three that you feel are crimes. What should be the punishment for each of them?

    Examples: fine (pay money)—how much?
    time in jail—how long?
    life in jail
    parole (leave jail early if you are good)
    capital punishment (killing)
    psychological help

    _____

    _____

    _____

    _____

2. Some countries have used the electric chair, stoning, whipping, and the sword as punishment. Are any of these used in your country? What do you think of them?

_____

_____

_____

3. Should all people get the same punishment for the same crime? Give an example for your answer.

_____

_____

_____

Part III

Share your answers with the whole class.

Write any new vocabulary or phrases that you learned in this discussion in the space below.

_____   _____

_____   _____

_____   _____

_____   _____

_____   _____

Activity 11

Take a Stand

In this discussion, you will think of ideas that people can agree or disagree with. Here are a few examples.

- People should not drink alcohol.
- A man should not marry a woman much older than he.
- If people are sick and want to die, they should be allowed to die.
- All students in my country should learn English.
- Couples shouldn't live together before they get married.
- It is better for parents to have male children.

Part I

In small groups, write a sentence on two topics that people can agree or disagree with. Here are some topics you might want to write a sentence about.

smoking	freedom
speed limit	taxes
government	AIDS
disabled people	T.V. commercials
T.V./movies	schools/this school
guns	environment
marriage	divorce
learning English	population control
men	women

You will need to choose two topics that everyone in the group can agree or disagree on. (If one person doesn't care about the topic, then choose another topic.) All students in a group should have the same two sentences.

1. _____

2. _____

Part II

Write your sentences on the board. After all the groups have put their sentences on the board, discuss them in your small group.

Give a number to each one:

    5 = I agree 100%
    4 = I agree 75%
    3 = I'm not sure
    2 = I disagree 75%
    1 = I disagree 100%

Explain why you agree or disagree.

Part III

(Optional) Choose one topic that you feel strongly about. Explain to the class why you feel the way you do. Begin your statements with "I agree because . . ." or "I disagree because . . . ."

Write any new vocabulary or phrases that you learned in this discussion in the space below.

_____   _____

_____   _____

_____   _____

_____   _____

_____   _____

Unit 2

Individual Speaking Activities

Activity 12

Introductions

You are going to interview another student and introduce him/her to the class. Take ten to fifteen minutes, and ask each other the following questions. Write down your answers.

1. Where were you born?

_____

_____

_____

_____

2. Why are you studying English?

_____

_____

_____

3. What do you want to do after you finish studying English?

_____

_____

_____

4. What's your favorite activity?

_____

_____

_____

5. What's your favorite dessert?

_____

_____

_____

6. If you could be a movie star or a famous athlete, who would you like to be? Why?

_____

_____

_____

_____

7. Ask at least one other question.

_____

_____

_____

_____

a. You can begin your talk by saying:

    I talked to _____. S/he is a very _____ (interesting, nice, funny) person. I want to introduce her/him to you.

b. Use the information you got from your interview and tell the class about your partner (but remember not to read the answers one by one).

c. You can finish your talk by saying:

    I'm glad I met _____, and I hope you get a chance to talk to him/her, too. Thank you.

Activity 13

Fifteen Years from Now

In this activity, you will tell about what you will be doing fifteen years from now. Here are some questions. Write down your ideas.

1. Will you be married? Will you be single?

   _____

   _____

   _____

   _____

2. If you are going to be married, will you have children? What will they look like? What will they act like? Describe your husband/wife. If you are single, will you have a partner? If so, describe that person. If you already have a family, what will they be doing fifteen years from now?

   _____

   _____

   _____

3. Will you be working? What job will you have? What kinds of duties will you have for your job?

_____

_____

_____

_____

4. Where will you be living? In what city/country? What will your apartment/house look like?

_____

_____

_____

_____

5. What hobbies/activities will you enjoy?

_____

_____

_____

_____

6. What will you look like?

_____

_____

_____

_____

7. What will be your biggest wish for the year _____ ?

_____

_____

_____

_____

8. Any other ideas about what you will be doing:

_____

_____

_____

_____

a. You can begin your talk by saying:

In the year _____, I will . . .

b. Tell about the answers you have (but remember not to read them one by one).

c. You can finish your talk by saying:

My biggest wish for the year _____ will

be _____

_____.

I hope I get it! Thank you.

Activity 14

Let Me Show You How . . .

In this activity, you will show or teach the class how to do something. Here are some ideas.

- cooking a food
- playing a musical instrument
- showing body language and its meaning in your country
- teaching a card trick
- solving a math problem or puzzle
- making something with paper (e.g., origami*)
- writing characters in another language
- using an abacus
- showing a costume from your country (e.g., thobe, kimono) and how to wear it
- showing how to do a sport or dance
- teaching some phrases from your language
- showing some phrases in sign language (language for the deaf)

* Japanese paper folding.

Choose something to show or teach the class.

a. You can begin your talk by saying:

I'm going to show you _____

_____. I learned how to do this

(tell who taught you or when you learned it).

b. *Show* the class how to do it. Try to do the activity in steps:

1st _____

_____

_____

2nd _____

_____

_____

3rd _____

_____

_____

etc.

(Remember to keep talking while you are showing.)

c. Give the class a chance to try, if possible.

d. You can finish your talk by saying:

I enjoy _____

because _____, and I

hope you try it and enjoy it, too. Thank you.

Activity 15

I Could Have Died!!!

Everyone has had a time when they felt very embarrassed or stupid. Maybe your face even turned red. Something happened, or you did something and you wanted to die!!

Think of a time when you **could have died** (you felt so embarrassed that you wanted to die).

a. Often, embarrassing things have happened to people when they were in elementary or high school. Perhaps you were out on a date with a boyfriend or girlfriend. Or maybe you remember something that happened when you were trying to speak English. Tell about your experience.

_____

_____

_____

_____

_____

_____

b. Tell the class how you felt. Also tell what your physical
   reactions were (what happened to your body). Here is some
   useful vocabulary: nervous, sweat, perspire, shake, blush,
   butterflies in your stomach, scared, laugh, cry.

   _____

   _____

   _____

   _____

   _____

   _____

c. Tell how the experience ended.

_____

_____

_____

_____

d. You can finish your talk by saying:

I could have died then, but now it's OK.

or

I could have died then, and I still feel that way!!
Thank you.

Activity 16

ESL/EFL Teacher for a Day

Imagine you are an ESL or EFL teacher for a speaking class. You can do anything you want. How would you teach English? What do you think would be the best way for your students to learn to speak English?

Write a few ideas (not complete sentences) for each of the following questions.

1. Would you give homework? How much? What kind?

   _____

   _____

   _____

   _____

2. How much discussion would there be in the class?

   _____

   _____

   _____

   _____

3. What would you do to encourage (help) students to speak?

   _____

   _____

   _____

   _____

4. How would you make the class interesting?

_____

_____

_____

_____

_____

5. How much listening practice would you have?

_____

_____

_____

_____

6. How would you arrange the desks or tables in the classroom? Draw a picture here.

7. What would be the best way for the students to work: in pairs, in small groups, in one large group? Why?

_____

_____

_____

8. Would your teaching style be strict or relaxed? Why?

_____

_____

_____

9. If students were late or absent a lot, what would you do?

_____

_____

_____

_____

10. If students spoke their own language in the classroom, what would you do?

_____

_____

_____

_____

11. What advice would you give students for meeting native speakers or hearing native speech?

_____

_____

_____

_____

12. In your opinion, what makes a good student?

_____

_____

_____

_____

   a. You can begin your talk by saying:
    The best way to teach speaking is to

_____

_____

b. Tell about the answers you have (but remember not to read them one by one).

_____

_____

c. You can finish your talk by saying:

I would enjoy/not enjoy teaching English because

_____

_____

Thank you.

Activity 17

My First Week

Think about your first week in the host country.

Here are some questions to ask yourself. Write a few *ideas* (not complete sentences) for each of the following.

1. What did you notice (see and remember) as you came off the airplane (or train, bus, etc.)?

_____

_____

2. Did anyone meet you? How did you feel? Were you nervous, excited, tired, confused, sad, happy, exhausted (very, very tired)?

_____

_____

_____

_____

3. What did you first notice (see and remember) in the city?

_____

_____

_____

_____

4. What was the first food you ate? What did you think?

_____

_____

_____

_____

5. How did you sleep? Did you have trouble with a time change?

_____

_____

_____

_____

6. Who did you stay with? Was it a good experience? Why or why not?

_____

_____

_____

_____

7. What did you think about the room, house, apartment, dorm, or place you stayed? Did you notice anything special or different about the bedroom, bed, bathroom, kitchen, or other rooms or furniture?

_____

_____

_____

_____

8. Did you bring what you needed? Did you forget anything or wish you had brought other things?

_____

_____

_____

_____

9. Did anything strange or funny happen to you? If yes, what?

_____

_____

_____

_____

10. Imagine you have a friend coming here. What advice (suggestions) would you give him/her?

_____

_____

_____

    a. You can begin your talk by saying:

       My first week was very _____

       because _____

       _____

    b. Tell about the answers you have (but remember not to read them one by one).

c. You can finish your talk by saying:

Now I have been here _____

and I feel _____

Thank you.

Activity 18

Picture Show

In this activity, you will use pictures to tell the class about your family or the city you are from.

Family

For this activity you will need pictures of your family. (If you like to draw, you can draw pictures of them.) Tell the class about your family. Use the following information to help you prepare your talk.

1. names of the people in your family

   _____

   _____

   _____

   _____

2. where you are in the family (for example: first child, youngest, parent)

   _____

   _____

   _____

   _____

3. parents/how they met (If you are married, tell about your partner and how you met.)

   _____

   _____

   _____

   _____

4. what each person in your family is doing now

_____

_____

_____

_____

5. interests/hobbies/clubs for each person

_____

_____

_____

_____

6. your relationship with your family

_____

_____

_____

_____

7. pets in your family

_____

_____

_____

_____

a. You can begin your talk by saying:

I'm happy to tell you about my family because

_____

_____

b. You can finish your talk by saying:

You can't meet them in person, but I hope these pictures helped you to know them. Thank you.

City

Imagine we are visiting your city for the first time. Take us on a tour.

1. What should we see?

_____

_____

_____

_____

2. Where should we visit?

_____

_____

_____

_____

_____

3. What are the most interesting places during the day?
   At night?

_____

_____

_____

_____

_____

If these questions are difficult for you to answer about your own city, take us on a tour of a nearby city that would be easier for you to talk about. Use pictures to show us the places. If you don't have pictures, you can go to the library and try to find some books that have pictures.

a. You can begin your talk by saying:

I'm going to take you on a picture tour of _____.

It's a very _____ place/city because _____

_____

b. You can finish your talk by saying:

I hope someday you can come to _____ and

take a tour in person! Thank you.

Activity 19

Radio Show

In this activity, you are going to make a radio show of about ten minutes. You can talk about anything you want in your show. Here are some topics.

- weather
- news
- traffic
- commercials (that you make up)
- interviews
- sports
- music (no more than three minutes!)

a. Write down other topics you can think of.

_____

_____

_____

_____

b. Work in small groups of three to four students. Decide what you want to have in your show. Make a list of topics. Next to each topic, write the name(s) of who will work on it. Each person should prepare that topic and speak for at least one minute. Listen to radio stations at different times of the day to get ideas.

_____

_____

_____

_____

c. Choose a name for your station. Also, choose one person to be the disc jockey and help that person prepare his/her role.

d. When you are ready, record the show on cassette. Your teacher will tell you what day to bring the cassette to class and play it for the other students.

e. Some hints for a good radio show:

   • Try not to have all your music at the beginning and all the talking afterwards. Blend (mix) the talking with the music.

   • It's more interesting for the class if you play parts of several songs, rather than one song completely. Three minutes is a long time to listen!

- When you end a song, turn it down slowly rather than stopping it suddenly. When you begin a song, turn it up slowly while you finish talking.

- Use vocabulary that everyone knows. Remember, the audience can't read what you are saying, and because of differences in students' pronunciation, hard words will be difficult for everyone to understand.

- Remember to have a conclusion. Instead of saying "That's all" or just stopping the show, thank the audience for listening, or say it's time for you to leave and you hope they will listen again. Listen to shows on the radio to get ideas for how to finish.

- Play the cassette in the classroom before you play it for the class to check the sound quality.

Unit 3

Interviews

Activity 20

Have You Ever . . . ?

In this activity, you are going to interview other students in your class and find out special information about them.

Part I

Ask anyone in class the first question. If s/he says "no," keep asking until you find someone who can answer "yes." Write down what the person says (you don't need to write complete sentences) and his/her name. Then ask another person the next question.

1. Have you ever seen or talked to a famous person?

   Who? _____

   Where? _____

   What did you say to him or her? _____

   _____

   _____
   (name)

2. Have you ever won a prize?

   What for? _____

   What did you win? _____

   _____
   (name)

3. Have you ever had a scary experience?

   Tell about it. _____

   _____

   _____
   (name)

4. Have you ever had a job you loved (or hated)?

   What was it? _____

   Why was it wonderful/terrible? _____

   _____

   _____
   (name)

5. Have you ever lost something very important?

What? _____

When? _____

What happened? _____

_____
(name)

6. Have you ever had a wish come true?

What? _____

When? _____

_____
(name)

7. Have you ever been in love?

When? _____

With who? _____

What happened? _____

_____

_____
(name)

8. Have you ever had a broken heart?

Why? _____

_____

_____
(name)

9. Have you ever been in an accident?

What happened? _____

_____

                                    _____
                                          (name)

10. Have you ever stayed up for more than twenty-four hours?

Why? _____

_____

                                    _____
                                          (name)

11. Have you ever felt very embarrassed?

Why? _____

_____

                                    _____
                                          (name)

12. Have you ever gotten very upset or angry?

Why? _____

How did you show you were angry?

_____

                                    _____
                                          (name)

Part II

When you are finished, tell the class about an answer s/he got. Now you have special information about the people in your class.

Part III

(Optional) Make a class book. Collect pictures of your classmates. Paste the pictures on paper and write some of the information that you got next to each picture.

Activity 21

Popular Culture

In this activity, you are going to find out what people in your area think is the most popular (what everybody likes).

Part I

For each question, ask two different people. Write down their answers. Also ask them to sign their name at the end of the interview. Practice the questions in class with a partner first, so that you don't need to read them when you speak.

1. Who is the most popular actor/actress?

   #1 _____ #2 _____

2. What is the most popular T.V. show?

   #1 _____ #2 _____

3. Who is the most popular athlete?

   #1 _____ #2 _____

4. What is the best fast food restaurant?

    #1 _____ #2 _____

5. a. What is the most popular song?

    #1 _____ #2 _____

    b. Who is the most popular singer?

    #1 _____ #2 _____

6. What is the most popular tourist attraction in the area?

    #1 _____ #2 _____

7. What is the most popular car?

#1 _____ #2 _____

8. What is the favorite holiday in your country?

#1 _____ #2 _____

_____   _____
(signature)   (signature)

Part II

As a class, make a list of the answers. Some students can make a list of all the answers for #1. Other students can make a list of all the answers for #2. Put the answers in order from most popular to least popular. Then make a final list of the top answer for each question. Now you know what people in the area think is the most popular.

Part III

(Optional) Which answers surprised you? Why? Did you learn anything new?

Activity 22

International Trivia

Part I

Ask two people the following questions. You will need to make complete sentences for numbers two through ten. Practice the questions in class with a partner first, so that you don't need to read them when you speak.

1. Who/first astronaut/walk on the moon?

    #1 _____ #2 _____

2. What/highest mountain/North America?

    #1 _____ #2 _____

3. What culture invented paper?

    #1 _____ #2 _____

4. What/second longest river/world?

    #1 _____ #2 _____

5. What and where/largest desert/world?

    #1 _____ #2 _____

6. How many provinces/in Canada?

    #1 _____ #2 _____

7. Where/biggest earthquake/twentieth century?

#1 _____ #2 _____

8. What/biggest ocean/world?

#1 _____ #2 _____

9. Where/1988 Winter Olympics?

#1 _____ #2 _____

10. What company/C.D. (compact disk) invented?

#1 _____ #2 _____

_____   _____
(signature)   (signature)

Answers are on p. 164.

Part II

_____

_____ *Trivia*

In small groups, write six questions about your country or the world (write complete sentences). Interview two people and write their answers.

1. _____

2. _____

3. _____

4. _____

5. _____

6. _____

ANSWERS

1. _____   1. _____

2. _____   2. _____

3. _____   3. _____

4. _____   4. _____

5. _____   5. _____

6. _____   6. _____

_____   _____
(signature)   (signature)

Part III

Choose a few of the questions and answers and share them with the class.

Activity 23

Which Do You Like Better?

Part I

In this interview, you need to find a *different* person (not in your class) for each question. Ask each person which they like better. Then ask them why. Write down their ideas (you don't need to write a complete sentence for each).

Practice the questions in class with a partner first, so that you don't need to read them when you speak. Remember to get signatures.

1. a busy weekend/a quiet weekend

   Why? _____

   _____
   (signature)

2. watching videos/going to a movie

   Why? _____

   _____
   (signature)

3. sleeping eight hours/sleeping more than eight hours/sleeping less than eight hours

   Why? _____

   _____
   (signature)

4. going to a casual restaurant/going to a fancy restaurant

   Why? _____

   (Which restaurant in the area do you recommend?) _____

   _____

   _____
   (signature)

5. eating chicken and fish/eating red meat

   Why? _____

   _____
   (signature)

6. buying a new car/buying a used car

   Why? _____

   _____
   (signature)

7. eating breakfast/skipping breakfast

   Why? _____

   _____
   (signature)

8. traveling in this country/traveling abroad

Why? _____

(Where do you recommend traveling to?) _____

_____

_____
(signature)

9. using a typewriter/using a computer/writing by hand

Why? _____

_____
(signature)

10. _____
(ask your own question)

Why? _____

_____
(signature)

Part II

In class, tell about some of the answers you got. Are there any that were surprises for you? Which ones?

Activity 24

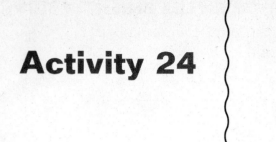

Riddles

Part I

Here are some riddles. Find five people not in your class and ask each one a different question. Practice the questions in class with a parter first, so that you don't need to read them when you speak.

(Optional) Ask one or two people you interview to tell *you* a riddle. Bring it to class and ask students to guess the answer.

1. A woman was born in India, raised in Japan, went to Europe, and died in Paris. What is she?

   _____
   (signature)

2. Do you say, "Thirty three and forty nine is eighty one" or "Thirty three and forty nine are eighty one"?

   _____
   (signature)

3. What does Canada produce more than any other country?

   _____
   (signature)

4. You are dreaming that you are on a mountain. A giant bear is coming toward you. There is no place to run to the left or right. You are against a wall. If you jump, you will die. How do you escape?

_____
(signature)

5. Where can you always find diamonds and gold?

_____
(signature)

Answers are on p. 164.

Part II

(Optional) In small groups, tell other students a riddle from your country. Choose one riddle from each group to ask the whole class.

Activity 25

Getting to Know You Better

Part I

In this interview, you will learn more information about your classmates. For each question, ask three different people.

1. How many people are there in your family? Are you the first born, in the middle, or the youngest?

a. _____   _____
        (answer)   (name)

b. _____   _____
        (answer)   (name)

c. _____   _____
        (answer)   (name)

d. _____   _____
        (answer)   (name)

e. _____   _____
        (answer)   (name)

2. Who do you look like—your father or your mother? How or in what way?

   a. _____

   (answer)

   _____

   (name)

   b. _____

   (answer)

   _____

   (name)

   c. _____

   (answer)

   _____

   (name)

3. What were you like as a child according to your family (what did your family say about you)?

   a. _____   _____

   (answer)   (name)

   b. _____   _____

   (answer)   (name)

   c. _____   _____

   (answer)   (name)

4. Do you or someone in your family have a special talent?

   a. _____   _____

   (answer)   (name)

   b. _____   _____

   (answer)   (name)

   c. _____   _____

   (answer)   (name)

5. Have you ever played a joke on someone, or do you know someone else who has? Tell about it.

a. _____
      (answer)

 _____

 _____
      (name)

b. _____
      (answer)

 _____

 _____
      (name)

c. _____
      (answer)

 _____

 _____
      (name)

6. What is one word that describes you?

a. _____   _____
         (answer)   (name)

b. _____   _____
         (answer)   (name)

c. _____   _____
         (answer)   (name)

Part II

Share your answers with the whole class.

Activity 26

In Your Country/ Hometown

Part I

Find students from other countries (or hometowns if you are all from the same country). Ask them the following questions about customs or traditions.

1. Do most people live in houses or apartments?

_____

_____
(name/place)

2. What holiday does your family like the best? Why? (Ask the person to explain the holiday if you don't know about it.)

    _____

    _____

    (name/place)

3. What food is very popular? (If you don't know about it, ask the person to explain it.)

    _____

    _____

    (name/place)

4. What do people usually wear when they are not working?

    _____

    _____

    (name/place)

5. What meals do families eat together?

_____

_____

(name/place)

6. What time do people go to work and come home?

_____

_____

(name/place)

7. How many hours a day do children go to school? How much time do they spend in after school activities and studying?

_____

_____

(name/place)

8. What religion is the most common?

_____

_____

(name/place)

9. What is the most common kind of transportation (e.g., car, bus, train)?

_____

_____)

(name/place)

10. What do people like to do on weekends?

_____

_____
(name/place)

11. How much vacation time a year do people usually have (both workers and students)?

_____

_____
(name/place)

12. How is the leader of your country chosen (or decided)?

_____

_____
(name/place)

Part II

After you have finished your interviews, come to class ready to answer the following questions.

1. Which answers were very different from your country/hometown?

   _____

   _____

   _____

2. Were there any answers that surprised you?

   _____

   _____

   _____

3. Tell the class something new that you learned.

   _____

   _____

   _____

Unit 4

Problem Solving Activities

Activity 27

Lost and Found?
A Logic Puzzle

Bill, Jill, Lil, and Will all went on a trip together. While on the trip, each one lost something: a wedding ring, a diamond watch, a pair of glasses, and a wallet.

With a partner, try to find out what each person lost. Here is some information, but be careful! Not all of the information will help you. (Use the chart to help you figure out the answer.)

1. One of the men is getting married in two weeks.
2. Two of the people are married to each other. One of them lost the wedding ring.
3. Lil doesn't own any jewelry.
4. One of the men doesn't like to spend money.
5. Jill's wedding ring is gold.
6. Bill's girlfriend doesn't like to travel.
7. Will's partner is the only one with poor eyesight.
8. Lil travels often.
9. Everybody who is married has a wedding ring.

	ring	watch	glasses	wallet
Bill				
Jill				
Will				
Lil				

The answer is on p. 165.

Activity 28

Wanted: One Wife

Read the ad on page 128 and then ask your teacher questions to find the answers. (Teacher: please see notes.) This is good practice for *wh*-questions.

Jack wants a wife. He put an ad in the newspaper.

> **Wanted**: One wife; young, thin, medium height, dark eyes, dark hair

Five women answered the ad. Which one did he choose?

name	age	weight	height	eyes	hair
Sue	19				
Kay	50 kg.	110 lbs.			
Jean		168 cm.	5'6"		
Elle				brown	
Kim					brown

Example: How old is Sue?   19.

Activity 29

A Lazy Guy

Read the story and then ask your teacher questions to find the answers. (Teacher: please see notes.) This is good practice for the present perfect tense.

> I have an easy life. I'm a millionaire. I have never worked.
> I have never been married. I have had many girlfriends. I
> have traveled around the world many times. I have just
> bought my tenth sports car. I think I have had a good life,
> but some people say I'm lazy.

WHO AM I?

name	job	marriage	girlfriends	travel	car
Tom	no				
Dick		no			
Jack			yes		
Bill				yes	
Bob					yes
Peter					

Example: Has Tom ever worked? No.

Activity 30

Pronunciation Pairwork: Difficult Consonants

Here are some phrases you need to practice before doing the following activities.

<u>underline</u>
circle
put an X on
put a check ✔ next to

Example:

Underline the word *turtle*.

table <u>turtle</u> title

Circle the word *turtle*.

table (turtle) title

Put an X on the word *turtle*.

table ~~turtle~~ title

Put a ✔ next to the word *turtle*.

table turtle ✔ title

Partner A

For the shaded words, tell your partner which words to mark. For the unshaded words, follow your partner's instructions. (Be careful not to look at your partner's page!)

Here are some phrases you need to give instructions:

<u>underline</u>
circle
put an X on
put a check ✔ next to

1. *l/r*   Give instructions to your partner.

| liver | lock | hill | <u>store</u> | crowd |
| river | rock | ~~hear~~ | stole | cloud |

(liver is circled, lock is underlined, hear is crossed out, store is underlined, cloud is circled)

2. *th/s/z*   Listen to your partner's instructions and mark the words you hear.

| mouth | think | Sue | ice | breeze |
| mouse | sink | zoo | eyes | breathe |

3. *b/v/f/p*   Give instructions to your partner.

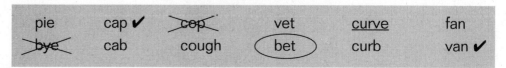

| pie | cap ✔ | ~~cop~~ | vet | <u>curve</u> | fan |
| ~~bye~~ | cab | cough | bet | curb | van ✔ |

(cap has a check, cop is crossed out, bye is crossed out, bet is circled, curve is underlined, van has a check)

4. *sh/ch/j*   Listen and mark.

| chip | wash | jeep | cheap | jeep |
| ship | watch | sheep | sheep | cheap |

(Optional) Take a minute and mark the ***unshaded*** words on your paper (any way you like). Give Partner B your instructions.

Partner B

For the shaded words, tell your partner which words to mark.
For the unshaded words, follow your partner's instructions. (Be
careful not to look at your partner's page!)

Here are some phrases you need to give instructions:

underline
circle
put an ✕ on
put a check ✔ next to

1. *l/r*   Listen and mark.

liver	lock	hill	store	crowd
river	rock	hear	stole	cloud

2. *th/s/z*   Give instructions to your partner.

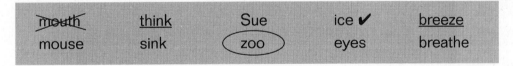

~~mouth~~	<u>think</u>	Sue	ice ✔	<u>breeze</u>
mouse	sink	(zoo)	eyes	breathe

3. *b/v/f/p*   Listen and mark.

pie	cap	cop	vet	<u>curve</u>	fan
bye	cab	cough	bet	curb	van

4. *sh/ch/j*   Give instructions to your partner.

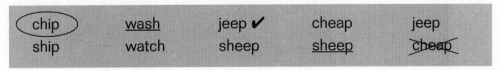

(chip)	<u>wash</u>	jeep ✔	cheap	jeep
ship	watch	sheep	<u>sheep</u>	~~cheap~~

(Optional) Take a minute and mark the ***unshaded*** words on your
paper (any way you like). Give Partner A your instructions.

Activity 31

Pronunciation Pairwork: Difficult Vowels

Here are some phrases you need to practice before doing the following activities.

underline
circle
put an ✗ on
put a check ✔ next to

Example: Underline the word *turtle*.

table   <u>turtle</u>   title

Circle the word *turtle*.

table   (turtle)   title

Put an ✗ on the word *turtle*.

table   ~~turtle~~   title

Put a ✔ next to the word *turtle*.

table   turtle ✔   title

Partner A

For the shaded words, tell your partner which words to mark.
For the unshaded words, follow your partner's instructions. (Be
careful not to look at your partner's page!)

Here are some phrases you need to give instructions:

underline
circle
put an ✕ on
put a check ✔ next to

1. i/ɪ   *(meet/mitt)* Give instructions to your partner.

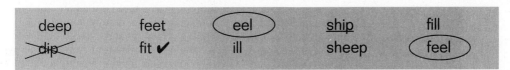

| deep | feet | ~~eel~~ (circled) | ship (underlined) | fill |
| ~~dip~~ | fit ✔ | ill | sheep | feel (circled) |

2. ɪ/ɛ/ə   *(bit/bet/but)* Listen and mark.

| mitt | hear | money | bell | ton | one |
| mutt | hair | many | bill | ten | win |

3. æ/a/ə   *(pat/pot/putt)* Give instructions to your partner.

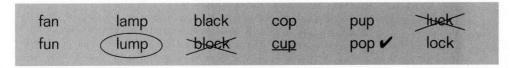

| fan | lamp | black | cop | pup | ~~luck~~ |
| fun | lump (circled) | ~~block~~ | cup (underlined) | pop ✔ | lock |

4. ɛ/æ/ə/e   *(bet/bat/but/bait)* Listen and mark.

| send | bank | rain | paint | ankle | men |
| sand | bunk | ran | pant | uncle | man |

(Optional) Take a minute and mark the ***unshaded*** words on your
paper (any way you like). Give Partner B your instructions.

Partner B

For the shaded words, tell your partner which words to mark. For the unshaded words, follow your partner's instructions. (Be careful not to look at your partner's page!)

Here are some phrases you need to give instructions:

<u>underline</u>
circle
put an ✗ on
put a check ✔ next to

1. i/ɪ   *(meet/mitt)* Listen and mark.

deep	feet	eel	ship	fill
dip	fit	ill	sheep	feel

2. ɪ/ɛ/ə   *(bit/bet/but)* Give instructions to your partner.

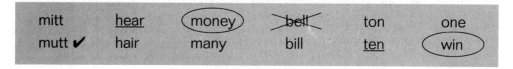

3. æ/a/ə   *(pat/pot/putt)* Listen and mark.

fan	lamp	black	cop	pup	luck
fun	lump	block	cup	pop	lock

4. ɛ/æ/ə/e   *(bet/bat/but/bait)* Give instructions to your partner.

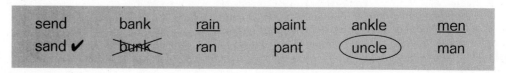

(Optional) Take a minute and mark the **unshaded** words on your paper (any way you like). Give Partner A your instructions.

Activity 32

Pronunciation Pairwork: Numbers and Letters

Here are some phrases you need to practice before doing the following activities.

<u>underline</u>
circle
put an ✕ on
put a check ✔ next to

Example: Underline the word *turtle*.

table   <u>turtle</u>   title

Circle the word *turtle*.

table   (turtle)   title

Put an ✕ on the word *turtle*.

table   ~~turtle~~   title

Put a ✔ next to the word *turtle*.

table   turtle ✔   title

Partner A

For the shaded words, tell your partner what to mark. For the unshaded words, follow your partner's instructions. (Be careful not to look at your partner's page!)

Here are some phrases you need to give instructions:

<u>underline</u>
circle
put an ✕ on
put a check ✔ next to

1. Give instructions to your partner.

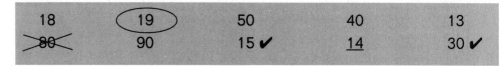

| 18 | ⃝ 19 ⃝ | 50 | 40 | 13 |
| ~~80~~ | 90 | 15 ✔ | <u>14</u> | 30 ✔ |

2. Listen and mark.

| A a | E e | I i | G g | U u |
| J j | Z z | W w | V v | X x |

3. Give instructions to your partner.

| 117 | ⃝ 170 ⃝ | <u>160</u> | 116 |
| 1017 ✔ | 1016 | 11⃝70⃝ | ~~1117~~ |

4. Listen and mark.

| U u | Y y | H h | L l | R r |
| B b | F f | V v | P p | Q q |

(Optional) Take a minute and mark the **_unshaded_** words on your paper (any way you like). Give Partner B your instructions.

Partner B

For the shaded words, tell your partner which words to mark.
For the unshaded words, follow your partner's instructions. (Be careful not to look at your partner's page!)

Here are some phrases you need to give instructions:

underline
circle
put an X on
put a check ✔ next to

1. Listen and mark.

18	19	50	40	13
80	90	15	14	30

2. Give instructions to your partner (in any order).

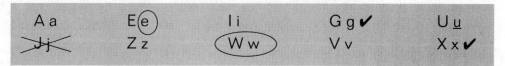

A a	E e	I i	G g ✔	U u
J j	Z z	W w	V v	X x ✔

3. Listen and mark

117	170	160	116
1017	1016	1170	1117

4. Give instructions to your partner (in any order).

U u	Y y	H h	L l	R r ✔
B b	F f ✔	V v	P p	Q q

(Optional) Take a minute and mark the **unshaded** words on your paper (any way you like). Give Partner A your instructions.

Activity 33

The Chillworth Mystery

In this activity, you will try to solve a mystery. Read the story and study the clues. Try to find out *who killed Sir Chillworth.*

According to the police report, Lady Chillworth called the police at 7:30 P.M. Her husband was lying on the bedroom floor. Someone had hit him on the head many times. He was dead, probably since 6:30 P.M.

Who killed Sir Chillworth? Here are the clues:

- When the police arrived, Mrs. Chillworth wasn't crying.
- The month before, the Chillworth home had been robbed. Sir Chillworth saw the robber running away. He thought he had seen the robber's face before.

- Sir Chillworth was a mean, unkind man. His employees hated him. One of them, Furney, said "I hope he dies soon." Furney didn't come to work the day Chillworth died.

- Lady Chillworth said she had been cooking a chicken dinner in the kitchen from 5:45 to 7:00 P.M. Cooking was her hobby.

- A servant had been fired by the Chillworths the week before. He had an extra key to the house. A gun was found in his room.

- Several drops of water were found around the head of Sir Chillworth.

- Sir Chillworth had two girlfriends, Rachel and Serena. Serena had recently found out about Rachel. Chillworth told Serena he was going to marry Rachel. The police found a hammer in Serena's car. There was no blood on it.

- Sir Chillworth told his wife one week before his death that he wanted a divorce.

- Lady Chillworth was very friendly to the police officers. She even gave them some chicken to take back to the station.

- A ladder was found next to the bedroom window.

Back at the police station, Officer Hines was thinking about the case. Why wasn't Lady Chillworth crying? She seemed like a nice lady, but not a great cook. Too bad the chicken wasn't cooked enough.

He continued thinking about the case. So many people seemed to have a reason to kill Sir Chillworth. Then suddenly he knew the person and the murder weapon. He went and arrested (took to jail) _____
                                            (name)

In small groups, take fifteen to twenty minutes and give a reason why each person did or didn't kill Sir Chillworth.

Robber: _____

Servant: _____

Furney: _____

Serena: _____

Rachel: _____

Lady Chillworth: _____

The answer is Lady Chillworth. Now try to figure out how Officer Hines knew she did it and what murder weapon she used.

Write down the clues about her below:

_____

_____

_____

_____

_____

_____

_____

You can find the answer on p. 167.

Brain Teasers

With a partner, try to solve the following puzzles.

1. What is the first shape in the following group:

   _____   ⧈   ⊃⊂   ⊂⊃   ⪫⪪

2. Using the numbers 1–9, put them in the squares so that the total for each row is 15.

15	15	15	15	15
15				15
15				15
15				15
15	15	15	15	15

3. Use each of the following

  +   –   ✕

  so that the numbers

  99   99   99 = 99.

4. Mr. Taller has a daughter. Who is taller? Mr. Taller or his daughter?

Answers are on p. 167.

Appendix

How to Begin and End an Interview

When you want to interview a person you do not know, here is a good way to begin:

Excuse me, I'm doing a homework assignment. Can I ask you a few questions?

When the interview is finished, you can say:

Thank you very much.
  or
Thank you for your time.

Notes to the Teacher

General Notes

Grammar Correction

As stated in the Preface, students need opportunities to simply talk. Some students have been exposed to such rigid grammar instruction that they are unable to say complete sentences without stopping. While grammar instruction has its place, too much of a focus on it can hinder fluency. Teachers wishing to address grammar may want to note common student errors and go over them when the discussion is finished, or at designated points in the discussion.

Monitoring Students

When students are in small groups, it is not possible for the teacher to listen to all students at all times. However, if fluency is the goal, *not* having the teacher present at all times may encourage students to speak more freely. *Self-monitoring* is one way to make the students more responsible for their speaking, especially when the class is large. One way to encourage this is to pass out the following self-evaluation to each student after the discussion.

This evaluation may be photocopied for classroom use.

DISCUSSION SELF-EVALUATION

_____
(name)

1. I spoke	often	sometimes	not much
2. I asked questions of other students.	often	sometimes	not much
3. I let other students talk.	often	sometimes	not much
4. I felt comfortable in my group.	yes a little no	Why or why not? _____

_____

_____

The form can be collected and, if appropriate, incorporated into the student's overall grade.

A Note About Group Processes

Working in groups is not always comfortable and both the teacher and students need to be aware that this is not an unusual feeling. Students may not get along, and some students may tend to dominate, while others may try to slide by. Students need to know that they will always encounter people they don't want to work with and that the challenge is to find ways to make it more comfortable.

Suggestions for Using the Activities in EFL Situations

If students are all from the same country or are learning English in their native country, the activities below can be modified. Listed are suggestions the instructor may wish to follow.

- **Activity 1:** *Ideas about a Country*
  Students can write ideas about the town they are living in or the town they came from, particularly if several students are from the same hometown.

- **Activity 17:** *My First Week*
  Students can talk about their first week in English class, or their first week in a city that they have visited on a trip.

- **Activity 18:** *Picture Show: City*
  Students can take the class on a tour of another city they have visited or would like to visit. This could involve visits to the library or possibly a travel agency in preparation for the talk.

- **Activity 26:** *In Your Country/Hometown*
  If students are all from the same area, assign them different countries. Have them go to the library and find out as much information as they can about their assigned country. When they do the interview in class, provide tags of the countries for them to wear so the country is easily identifiable.

Unit I: Discussions

The discussions are designed to take a minimum of fifty minutes; however, those students who need follow-up activities may require another class period.

Suggested Formats:

a. Students first discuss in groups of three to four students and then share their answers with the whole class. This can be very structured: One student is appointed leader and the other students answer. A student can even take the role of secretary and record the group's answers.

   When the entire class comes together, each student in the group can be assigned a question to report on.

b. Students discuss in pairs for ten to fifteen minutes. Two pairs are then put together so that four students talk. Finally, the entire class comes together for a brief sharing of ideas.

c. The entire class discusses the topic, with one student appointed the leader or several students taking turns, for example, every ten minutes. This format is not suggested when there are several students in the class who tend to dominate.

d. Conversation circle: The class is divided in half and makes two circles, one inside the other. The outer circle will rotate in the same direction. Two students opposite one another (one from each circle) talk about a question from the discussion. After a few minutes the outer circle rotates one person, and a new pair discusses the same question. This continues until there have been three or four rotations. On the fourth or fifth rotation, students discuss the next question.

Although it may seem repetitious to discuss the same question several times, students often find that they get better at it as they go along. They can practice expressing their ideas, and pick up ideas by talking or listening to other students.

Pairing of Students

In order to create a safe atmosphere for the quieter students to talk, have students work in pairs. One option is to pair a more talkative student with a quieter student if the talkative student is assigned the role of questioner. Or, two quieter students can work together.

Groups that Finish Early

In small group work, some groups occasionally finish early. The teacher can write additional questions on the board for students to answer or encourage students to practice what they will report to the entire class. This way they can check with other group members to clarify what they discussed.

Vocabulary

The students in your class may be at a range of levels. The following vocabulary is only *suggested*; you may find many words too high and some already familiar to your students.

Please note that each discussion is followed by a vocabulary section where students can write any new words they learned. You might want to tell students before the discussions to listen for and ask about new vocabulary.

The vocabulary in italics is already in the textbook but may be unknown to students.

Individual Discussion Activity Notes

- **Activity 1: *Ideas about a Country***
  If the class is taught in an EFL setting, please see p. 151 for
  suggestions on modifying this activity.

Vocabulary

> *jewelry (ring, necklace)*
> *respect (obey, follow, honor)*
> *violent (beat, hit, fight)*

A more advanced group may want to discuss:

stereotype	prejudice
bigotry	racism
labels	bias
discrimination	

Suggested Variation for Part II

Part II can be done for homework. When students come to class,
they can put their lists on the board. The teacher can lead a
discussion by asking questions about the stereotypes listed. For
example, if a student writes: "Italians are romantic," the teacher
can encourage students to explore this further by asking: "What
does romantic look like? What do you see when you think of
romantic Italians?"

The class could also explore the different "minority" groups in
the country they are visiting or living in.

Written Expansion

- *The country I have many stereotypes (ideas) about is* _____
  _____. (Give examples of stereotypes.)
- Write about stereotypes you had and if they have changed since this discussion.

- **Activity 2:** *Body Language*

Vocabulary

close (near, opposite of far away)

point	misunderstanding
express	nonverbal
expression	eye contact
facial expression	hug
frown	bear hug
wink	assertive
grin	pushy
rude	awkward
impolite	annoying
informal	obnoxious
misunderstand	

Notes about Part I

A person in the U.S. may indicate something is stupid by rolling their eyes.

Students in the U.S. may show their interest in a class by looking at the teacher, leaning forward, nodding, answering and asking questions, or being active in discussions.

Written Expansion

- *Three new things I learned about body language are . . .*
- Compare differences and similarities in body language between your country and the host country.

Additional Questions for Discussion

1. How do people show other emotions, for example, excitement or sadness?
2. How do people use their voice to show different feelings? (Students have commented to me that they can tell when Americans are angry because they use a clipped tone when speaking.)

3. What do you think about parents hugging or kissing their children?
4. What do you think about parents kissing each other or showing affection in front of the family?

- **Activity 3: *Dating, Marriage, and Divorce***

Vocabulary

> *blind date (someone else plans the meeting)*
> *chaperone (a person to go with the couple on the date)*
> *honeymoon (a trip after the wedding)*

partner	ex-wife
get married to	ex-husband
engagement	get divorced from
fiancé	separated

In answering number 6, the teacher may want to include a discussion about how to make small talk as a way to meet someone.

Written Expansion

- *The kind of wedding I want to have is . . .*
- *The perfect date for me is . . .*
- *When I am married, I hope . . .*

- **Activity 4: *Customs***
The teacher can help students brainstorm by writing the following topics on the board:

climate	food
transportation	TV
immigration	movies
friends	shopping
schools	banking
housing (house/apartment/dorm)	

Ask them what they find strange or difficult about any of the above.

Vocabulary

manners	uncommon
behavior	usual
rules	unusual
polite	can't stand

impolite

comfortable

uncomfortable

foreign

common

have difficulty/trouble (+ ing)

accustomed to

strange

bizarre

traditional

Written Expansion

- *A custom that is very unusual to me is . . .*
- *A custom in my country that people wouldn't understand is . . .*
- *Three things I learned about another culture are . . .*
- *A subject that people in my county do not discuss is . . .*

- **Activity 5: *After Death***

Vocabulary

spirit (without a body, ghost)
honor (respect, love, obey)

funeral

ceremony

casket

coffin

cemetery

grave

bury

burial

cremate

cremation

ashes

reincarnation

soul

pray

purgatory

tomb

bones

destiny

Written Expansion

- *When people die . . .*
- *After I die, I . . .*
- *The ceremony I want to have when I die . . .*
- *I want to/don't want to know the day I will die because . . .*

- **Activity 6: *Advantages/Disadvantages***

Vocabulary

communicate

habit

routine

accent

translate

frustrated

meet
vocabulary
words
pronounce/pronunciation

get used to
get accustomed to
adjust

Written Expansion

- *The biggest advantage/disadvantage of _____ for me is . . .*

- **Activity 7: *What Makes a Good Partner?***

Vocabulary

share (divide with others)
fifty-fifty
half and half
kind/kindness
warmth
gentle/gentleness
funny

sense of humor
outgoing
shy
physical appearance
housemate

Written Expansion

- *The perfect partner for me is . . .*
- *I would/would not be a good partner for someone because . . .*

- **Activity 8: *The Perfect Job***

Vocabulary

ability
good at
bad at
skill
training
business
profession
occupation
company
firm
admire
employer
self-employed

boss
supervisor
paycheck
salary
income
wages
position
quit
fire
layoff
unemployed
strike/be on strike

Written Expansion

- *The perfect job for me would be . . .*
- *One job I could never do . . .*
- *I admire people who work as* _____ *because . . .*

- **Activity 9:** *Culture Shock*

Vocabulary

get used to	differences
get accustomed to	common
adjust to	uncommon
adapt to	immerse
frustration	react
emotions	reaction
up and down	lack of sleep
feel overwhelmed	insomnia
loneliness	fatigue
isolation	boredom
similar/similarities	

Teachers may want to point out that culture shock is a common phenomenon; students can expect to encounter symptoms at one point or another in their stay. They are not "strange" for feeling the way they do.

It is useful to point out to students that they don't necessarily have to go to another country to experience culture shock; just taking a trip or visiting another city can bring it on.

Some suggestions for students in culture shock:

- Don't compare your country and the host country by thinking "my country has _____ and this country doesn't, so my country is better." A more helpful way to compare is: "My country has _____ and this country has _____; both are *different*." Comparing in terms of good vs. bad can increase or prolong the culture shock.
- Talk to your friends about how you're feeling.
- Talk to people who have already had culture shock.
- Take a "break" from English; read some newspapers, magazines, or books in your language.
- Be aware that culture shock will not last forever.

When students return to their country, they are likely to experience culture shock once again. They have become accustomed to aspects of the host country that they may not find in their country. Or, they may want to discuss their experiences with their friends and find that people are not interested in hearing about them. Talking about culture shock is vital; having some understanding of what is happening makes it much easier to get through.

Written Expansion

- Write about your first week in the host country—what was strange, difficult, frustrating, etc.
- Write about your experience of culture shock (or if you had a friend who had culture shock, write about his/her experience).

- **Activity 10: *Crime and Punishment***

Vocabulary

weapon	just
gun control	unjust
DWI (driving while intoxicated)	injustice
dishonest	innocent
moral	guilty
immoral	judge
corrupt	court
corruption	convict
fair	jury
euthanasia	sentence
affair	prison
adultery	capital punishment
violence	

Written Expansion

- _____ *is not a crime because . . .*
- *Some reasons for crime are . . .*
- Write about an injustice that you know/heard about.

- **Activity 11: *Take a Stand***

Vocabulary

In my opinion . . .
I agree . . .

It's my feeling that . . .
I disagree . . .
That's an interesting idea but . . .
You've made a good point but . . .
I'm sorry, but I have to disagree.
I don't understand exactly what you mean.
I didn't follow that exactly.

Unit II: Individual Speaking Activities

To reduce anxiety about what to say or how to say it, these activities are structured so that by the time students have answered all the questions, they have, in effect, put together their short talk. Suggested introductions and conclusions are also provided because this is often an awkward task for students.

Let students know that they can use note-cards when they speak but they should not read word for word. Emphasize that while they are talking, they should not go through the questions one by one. Rather, they should use the questions to put together their talk and then speak from notes.

Written Expansion for Individual Speaking Activities

- Students can put the information in their short talk into writing.
- Students can choose to take notes on another student's talk and write about it.

Evaluation of Short Talks

There are advantages if students are involved in the evaluation process too. They have to pay attention to the speaker, and everyone receives the feedback of many rather than one person (the teacher). The teacher benefits by seeing how much the students understand their classmates, what they respond to in a speech, and what they consider important in the grading process.

This evaluation may be photocopied for classroom use.

SPEECH EVALUATION

1. Clear, understandable speaking	5 4 3 2 1
2. Eye contact (looked at all the audience)	5 4 3 2 1
3. Content (followed speech instructions, interesting, stayed on the topic)	5 4 3 2 1
4. Preparation (seemed like the speaker practiced the speech)	5 4 3 2 1
5. Overall grade	5 4 3 2 1

Comments: _____

_____

(5) very good   ↔   (1) not good

For lower levels, a simplified scale is suggested: 3 – 2 – 1
   3 = yes   2 = in the middle   1 = needs to improve much more

Individual Speaking Activity Notes

- **Activity 14: *Let Me Show You How . . .***
  It's important that students continue talking *while* they are showing the class their activity. It may be helpful for the teacher to give a talk first so students can get ideas for how to do this.

- **Activity 16: *ESL/EFL Teacher for a Day***
  The following vocabulary may be useful to students as they answer the questions:

quiet	studious
talkative	lazy
shy	pairs
outgoing	group
strict	circle
relaxed	

- **Activities 17 and 18:** *My First Week/Picture Show*
  If the class is taught in an EFL setting, please see p. 151 for suggestions on modifying this activity.

- **Activity 19:** *Radio Show*
  Suggest to students that the show will be more enjoyable and fun for the class if they put together news about their classmates, their teacher, or the school.

  This activity can largely be done outside of class; in fact, my experience has been that allowing more than three class periods for students to work on this can be an ineffective use of class time.

  The following form may be photocopied for classroom use.

RADIO SHOW EVALUATION

1. Clear, understandable speaking   5 4 3 2 1

2. Followed instructions   5 4 3 2 1

3. Interesting show   5 4 3 2 1

4. Overall grade   5 4 3 2 1

Comments: _____

_____

(5) very good   ↔   (1) not good

Unit III: Interviews

The interviews help students get to know the individuals in their class as they ask each other questions or work together on assigned tasks. They also encourage students to talk to people outside of class (native speakers where feasible) so that they can expand their use of English beyond the classroom.

Interview Procedure

It is helpful at the beginning of the term to give the students a schedule of when the interviews are due:

Example: Due: Sept. _____ International Trivia
                        (day)

              Oct. _____ Which do you like better?
                    (day)

When students are interviewing people *not* in their class, encourage them to practice first with their classmates. You can remind them that before they ask a question, they can study it for a moment, but that when they speak, they need to look at the other person.

Also, let them know that when they do the interview, they should not hand the paper to the person being interviewed and say, "Here, can you answer these questions?" Rather, *they* need to ask the questions.

When students finish the interviews, whether as an in-class activity or as homework, the teacher can call on students to report the information they gathered.

If students are interviewing other members of the class, a fun way to get the interview started is for them to interview people based on categories, such as:

1. a person not from your country
2. a person of the opposite sex
3. a person taller or shorter than you
4. a person with curly hair
5. a person with straight hair
6. a person you don't know very well

These categories are only suggested; the ones you select will depend, of course, on your students.

Interview Activity Notes

- **Activity 20: *Have You Ever . . . ?***
  This interview is recommended for the first week of class so that students can become acquainted with the people they will be spending the term with.

- **Activity 22: *International Trivia***
  You may want to take students to the reference section of the library to show them books that would be helpful in creating questions.

Rather than having students ask two people ten questions each, you could have them find ten people and ask each one a different question.

ANSWERS

1. Neil Armstrong
2. Mt. McKinley (Alaska)
3. Chinese
4. Amazon
5. Sahara, Africa
6. 10
7. Japan (1933, 8.9)
8. Pacific
9. South Korea
10. Sony and Philips

- **Activity 24:** *Riddles*
  If you have students come back with new riddles, collect them and type them up for the class to answer.

ANSWERS

1. Dead
2. Neither. 33 + 49 = 82
3. Canadian
4. Wake up
5. In the dictionary

- **Activity 25:** *Getting to Know You Better*
  This is a useful interview to use in the middle of the term as students may have formed friendships with particular students in the class and not interacted as much with others. By doing this activity, students are encouraged to get reacquainted with *all* their classmates.

- **Activity 26:** *In Your Country/Hometown*
  If the class is taught in an EFL setting, please see p. 151 for suggestions on modifying this activity.

In the post-interview discussion, you can expand the question on meals (number 5) by asking whether they eat with chopsticks, forks, knives, and spoons, and who cooks.

Unit IV: Problem Solving Activities

- ## Activity 27: *Lost and Found?—A Logic Puzzle*

ANSWERS

	ring	*watch*	*glasses*	*wallet*	*married**
Bill	no	yes	no	no	no
Jill	no	no	yes	no	yes
Will	yes	no	no	no	yes
Lil	no	no	no	yes	no

* It helps to add this category to solve the puzzle.

1. *Lil doesn't own any jewelry.* "No" for ring and watch for Lil.
2. *The people who are married have wedding rings.* So, she isn't married.
3. *Bill's girlfriend doesn't like to travel. Two of the people are married to each other. One of them lost the ring.* So, Will is the married person. His partner must be Jill.
4. *Will's partner is the only one with poor eyesight.* "Yes" for glasses for Jill.
5. *Two of the people are married to each other. One of them lost the ring.* Since Jill is "yes" for glasses, Will is "yes" for the ring.

With these clues, you now have enough information to fill in the rest of the grid with "yes" and "no."

(Sentences number 4 and number 8 of the puzzle are not useful to the answer.)

- **Activities 28 and 29:** *Wanted—One Wife / A Lazy Guy*
  One suggestion for the following two activities is to have students ask questions in teams.

- *Wanted—One Wife*

(For the weight and height, you can give the answer in the Metric System or the U.S. Customary System. To make it really challenging, you can alternate them— metric for one answer and U.S. for another.)

name	age	weight	height	eyes	hair
Sue	19	110 lb. 50 kg.	6'0" 183 cm.	brown	brown
Kay**	19	110 lbs. 50 kg.	5'5" 165 cm.	brown	brown
Jean	19	300 lb. 136 kg.	5'6" 168 cm.	brown	brown
Elle	89	110 lb. 50 kg.	5'6" 168 cm.	brown	brown
Kim	19	110 lb. 50 kg.	5'6" 168 cm.	blue	brown

**Answer

Conversions: 1 pound = 2.2 kg.
              1 inch   = 2.54 cm.

- *A Lazy Guy*

Who Am I?

name	job	marriage	girlfriends	travel	car
Tom	no	no	yes	yes	no
Dick	no	no	yes	yes	no
Jack	no	no	yes	no	yes
Bill**	no	no	no	yes	yes
Bob	no	no	no	yes	yes
Peter	yes	no	yes	yes	yes

** Answer

- **Activity 33: *The Chillworth Mystery***
Lady Chillworth hit her husband over the head with a frozen chicken (hence the drops of water near her husband). She then cooked the chicken for dinner.

- **Activity 34: *Brain Teasers***

ANSWERS

1. AA   (The first five letters of the alphabet put back to back)

2.
2	7	6
9	5	1
4	3	8

3. $9 \times 9 = 81$
   $9 + 9 = 18$
   $9 - 9 = \underline{\ 0}$
       99

4. His daughter because she is a *little Taller*.

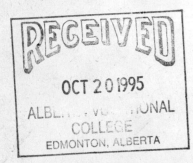